As-Is

HORSE RACING
THE ESSENTIAL GUIDE
TO BACKING
WINNERS
by
Sidney Harris

As-Is Publishing
www.as-is.co.uk

Horse Racing The Essential Guide to Backing Winners.

Published Dec. 1999.

Copyright© Sidney Harris. All Rights Reserved.

Published by **As-Is Publishing** 12 Prince Albert Street,
Brighton East Sussex, BN1 1HE. U.K   Phone: 01273 710109

                                                                        Fax: 01273 774820

                                                                                    www.as-is.co.uk

ISBN # 0 9537580 0-1

<u>Foreword</u>

"In an industry driven by betting and arguably run by bookmakers, if anyone is serious about having a bet, it is essential that they know the facts and understand the rules.

Yes! we have all had fun bets in our time and occasionally I'm guilty of doing so - but the fun is usually short-lived.

Sidney Harris' Essential Guide to Backing Winners, cuts out the painful process of having to encounter the pitfalls and goes on to enlighten the student in a clear and instructive way, judiciously reinforced by some appropriate quotations.

Sidney Harris pushes points where they need to be pushed and the bookmakers will not be overjoyed with him for doing so.

You need to be something of a chameleon to solve racing's colourful puzzles and this is the book to keep at hand while you do!"

– Mark J Polglase

"A fool and his money should never have got together to begin with!"
– *Gordon Gekko* Wall Street.

"Do you follow!"
– *Doyle Lonnegan* The Sting.

My acknowledgement to everyone who penned a quotation used in this book.   Sidney Harris.

Index

At the time of writing this book, I am in my seventh year as a Professional Gambler; within this time, no two years have been remotely the same. I became a Professional Gambler on 26/8/93 one day after the "Largest Bookmakers in the World" decided to prohibit my betting, as they thought, I was winning too much. Looking back at these seven years, I realise that I have been on both - a roller coaster ride and an acute learning curve.

The objective of this book is to clarify, beyond doubt, that the best way to find winners is through constant and consistent study, and that only by taking a methodical approach is it possible to make sense of the chaos that is unleashed the moment the starting stalls open for a horse race. In effect I want to give you the benefit of the learning curve without the upheaval of the roller coaster.

Many punters rely on luck, and in no instance is the saying: "The harder you work the luckier you get" more applicable than in horse racing. Each punter's journey is quite different, travelling an uncertain route without the benefit of a signpost. Entrenched misguided ideas, lead punters to repeat mistakes that eventually become debilitating and regularly indulged habits. Without a definite strategy, pinpointing mistakes becomes impossible. This book is about developing a common-sense strategy that takes many, not so obvious, winner finding options into account.

Horse Racing is fraught with financial danger. The childlike optimism of the punter is refreshed the moment he lays his hands on some newly acquired *Playing up money*. As the song says, "It's all about the money. "Punters on the whole get a terrible press. Perceived as: lazy ne'er do wells, driven by greed and looking to make easy money. Of course, none of us are keen to be included in this group. A visit to the betting shop at the end of *Lemming Lane* brings us in direct contact with the punters that swell the coffers of the bookmaking fraternity. Placepot junkies rubbing shoulders with odds-on aficionados, punters showing themselves no mercy, as every betting mistake is accomplished. Devoted to their own destruction they rush to compound their losses. The punter's day usually ends in a final frenzy when he panics to back the favourite in the last race. This last race of the day is cynically known as *"The get out stakes."* There's another quaint term in betting known as *"Leaving it behind."* The *it* in question, being the punter's money. Invariably when trying to balance his losses on the last race of the day - the punter does indeed leave *it* behind.

" One rarely sees how much one's in debt,
    until one comes to settle one's account." – *Goethe.*

In the Eyes of the Beholder

"Every handicap offers a premium to fraud, for horses are constantly started without intention of winning, merely to hoodwink the handicapper." Although the above are my sentiments, they are not my words - they are those of Admiral Henry Rous, the public handicapper of 100 years ago. The following is a recent statement made by Brigadier Roscoe Harvey, senior steward - while admonishing a jockey he suspected of not trying: "If you must pull a horse, which I don't recommend, you should keep your elbows moving to look as if you're trying."

There are penalties that have to be paid by trainer, jockey (and horse) for not trying, and we leave the legitimacy of the situation to the authorities. Our concern is, how we are affected in finding future winners, when we can't trust the form book 100%, as form cannot be taken literally if every horse in a race is not actually trying to win.

Much of my time is spent watching the Racing Channel for horses that are being *treated leniently* by their jockeys, my intention being to back them in the future when, hopefully, they will be attempting to win. There's an art in doing this. When watching a handicap race with an eye to a possible future winner, objectivity is the key. Video the race and watch it two or three times, you'll be surprised how little you picked up on in the first showing. I've watched many races half a dozen times before spotting which horse might be a probable winner in the near future.

Non Tryers

My fascination with handicap races is renewed every racing day. There is no doubt that the best betting value is to be found in handicaps, as we are looking for a winner in a race where, in effect, if the handicapper got it right and everybody was *playing the game*, we'd get an unfathomable photo finish. On his retirement, one of the greatest jockeys proffered this advice to any, up and coming, would be horse stopper: "If you want to get a horse stuffed, do all of the stuffing early on in the race - then give it the big finish." (Don't drop the anchor in the harbour, drop it out at sea.) In effect, a jockey following these instructions too fervently might well stop the horse and also pick up a ban for over use of the whip. But of course, there are *legitimate* ways of making sure a horse doesn't win until the time is considered right. Running on the wrong going, running at the wrong distance, running with heavyweight plates (horseshoes), running when over-trained or under-trained, running at the wrong track etc.

You are **not** dealing with a level playing field. As long as this is always remembered, you have a reasonable chance of finding winners.

Notwithstanding, the negativity, the form book remains your guide and touchstone, providing you read between the lines.

> "Jockeys ride to orders. If a horse is given an easy, it's due to orders, don't always single out the jockey"
> – *Michael Caulfield* - Jockey Association.

Shenanigans

"The great handicaps are productive of two thirds of the iniquities that disgrace the turf. To qualify a horse to win a handicap on a large scale it is considered necessary to deceive the handicapper by running him unprepared, by not allowing the horse to win for months, or even years. It is a very extraordinary occurrence for a horse to win in a handicap if he belongs to a fair trader" – *Admiral Rous*

Admiral Rous (The originator of the handicap) pulled no punches. I tend to think that one hundred years later racing is slightly more honest, with the emphasis on <u>slightly</u>.

Invariably when the major handicaps come around, on the flat or jumps, after the event you will hear that the winner had been laid out for the race. This of course means that the horse wasn't laid out, when he ran down the field a month ago, or for that matter when losing a month before that. Had you backed the horse in either of those races - are you entitled to feel robbed?

I believe you are entitled to feel robbed. In order not to fall victim again you have to cultivate your cynicism so that you expect some measure of evasive behaviour in racing.

I won't offer my own opinion on the current state of play. I'll leave that to the Master, whose opinions continue to stand the test of time:

"Fraud cannot be prevented by rules and regulations,
nor can you protect a person from having his pocket
picked by Act of Parliament." – *Admiral Rous.*

The Dodge

The dodge is a horse whose bare form could read something like this: 20322. It might well be the paper favourite today. You could well find that in its last run it was coming there nicely, on the bridle, but just didn't find enough to beat the winner. Look back through its form and you might discover, it once won a race; probably because the horse ahead of it stopped in its tracks. Usually relegated to second or third, the dodge makes the ideal false favourite as bookmakers recognise a dodge from the very first time it shrinks from putting its head in front.

Horses are inherently pack animals. If you watched the dodge at play, in a field full of horses, you would notice, although it seems to hold it's own, in the hierarchy, it will always shy away from the leader of the pack. When racing it assumes that the horse running at the front is the leader of the pack - and the dodge, by it's very nature doesn't challenge the leader's superiority. Look again through its form and you may well find that a jockey has incurred a whip ban on this horse. The dodge frustrates jockeys and trainers as much as it does punters.

I rarely have anything to do with betting each-way. But one of the few each-way bets I have ever had, was on a dodge that came second on the flat at 33/1. This horse had undoubted ability and went on to win races over hurdles as, having to concentrate on jumping it forgot its hang-up with the precepts of hierarchy.

"A deck of cards was built like the purest of hierarchies,
with every card a master to those below it." – Ely Culbertson.

The Knockout

To those of you who believe that a perfectly delivered knockout is best achieved with a short left hook, think again. Bookmakers are capable of delivering the smoothest knockouts. Whether the knockout is an art or a science is debatable. But when it's staged correctly - connections collect.

The scenario goes a little like this. Connections fancy their horse and believe defeat is out of the question. (A belief not to be recommended.) For the sake of this scenario we will assume that the horse is a second favourite in an egg and spoon race at a small track. The connections in question are smooth operators, wide boys of the old school, brought up in the game, faces of the first order. They intend backing their horse, but not at the track.They will be backing it in betting offices at the last minute.

At the track, connections have enlisted the help of a friendly bookmaker, whose job is to knockout the horse. Let's assume this horse is 7/2 in the papers and 3/1 on the tissue. The connection's bookmaker will take 4/1, 9/2, 5/1 and if possible 11/2 and 6/1. As we know, punters will shy away from this drifter, in fact this horse drifting will probably make them more inclined to back the favourite. Yes! you have the picture - It's an off course coup. Connections back the horse in the betting shops as late as possible, so that their money doesn't get back to the track and short circuit the ploy.

Always remember! Horses that drift are sometimes part of a greater plan.

The Tools of the Trade

The Racing Post every day, is your first essential. Used properly it will point you in the direction of winners. Other invaluable weekly publications are: The Racing Post Weekender and Raceform Update; which apart from building into form books are filled with information. Personally, I use computerised Raceform. There are other excellent computerised form books, i.e. Timeform and Superform just to mention the most popular. I find a regular form book, an essential supplement to computerised Raceform, it's preferable to use a separate source, as you get the benefit of a more objective view, with the benefit of two separate race readers and, of course, a third when you check the form in your daily Racing Post.

The more eclectic your information the more objective you can be. Another essential is Profile (racehorses & sires) published by Nomadic Press. (This is also published in computer versions for both national hunt and flat racing.) Profile has a wealth of information at a glance - covering track, distance, going and the time of year that a horse is likely to come to hand plus much more. Add to this, a subscription to the Racing Channel and the Racing Post Internet Site and you're on the way to taking horse racing very seriously.

"Knowledge advances by steps, and not by leaps" – *Macaulay.*

Essential Criteria

I'm sure that, occasionally, you'll break the following **Rules** –

...and wish you hadn't. They must be adhered to!

Never back a horse unproven on the going.

Never back a horse from a stable out of form.

Never back a horse unsuited to a track.

Never back a horse ridden by a jockey with a poor record at the track.

Never back a horse whose trainer has a poor record at the track.

Bookmakers look for horses with at least one of the above credentials as they make wonderful false favourites. Punters who can see no further than the favourite, find themselves backing these horses.

Having eliminated the above horses from a race you will have narrowed the field and saved yourself looking at the form of horses that can be immediately discounted. Statistically horses with the above negatives rarely win races. In effect, the only horses you are interested in backing must satisfy these **ESSENTIAL CRITERIA** first.

Any favourite that doesn't fulfil any of these **Essential Criteria** will be opposable with the **Reverse Book**, which is explained later.

"When you have eliminated the impossible, whatever remains however improbable, must be the truth."

– Sir Arthur Conan Doyle.

Accentuate the Positive

We are looking to back trainers in form; they're easy enough to find! Turn to Today's Trainers in your Racing Post and you will quickly be able to assess if a stable is in form.

We are looking to back trainers with a good record at a track! Turn to Top Trainers, at the track in question, in your Racing Post and you'll see at a glance which trainers are likely to be in contention.

We are looking to back jockeys, who have a good record at the track! Turn to Top Jockeys, at the track in question, in your Racing Post and you'll see at a glance which jockeys regularly do the business at this track. This narrowing down process has to be undertaken before looking at a horses form. It's unwise to look at the form of a horse first, as it might prematurely make a case for itself and ruin our objectivity.

When a horse has multiple future entries, it's a useful positive factor. This information is easy to ascertain. In Monday's Racing Post there's an Entries Index and another one in Wednesday's Weekender. A trainer looking for the right race will enter a horse in various races. These horses with multiple entries need added scrutiny. Look at the races they might have run in, as invariably, if the races they have been pulled out of are of a higher grade they then become more interesting.

"Eliminate the negative, Latch on to the affirmative and don't mess with mister-in-between." – *Johnny Mercer.*

A Race is a Race is a Race

So far, I've made no distinction between flat and jumps racing, or the type of race we're looking to be involved in. Realistically, a 4/1 Ascot group winner pays the same as a 4/1 winner in a lowly selling race at Newton Abbot. Making hard and fast rules about not backing in Ladies Races or Amateur Claiming Races etc. need not apply!

Assuming you follow the rules about **Essential Criteria**, you're not going to find yourself involved in any race that needs avoiding.

As you read on, you'll find that I've profiled each track individually, flat and jumps. The big distinction over the jumps is that the bookies have the added advantage of a horse falling in their favour. (Over 10% of National Hunt horses are brought down, fall or are pulled up) the only way this can be compensated for is by making sure you avoid horses that have too many falls in their history and ensure you never contemplate taking a short price in hurdles or chases. Fear of big field handicaps is absolutely unnecessary. Using the **Essential Criteria**, we've already established, you'll narrow the field considerably even before you start studying form in depth. The races I'm most likely to avoid are of six runners or less, where jockey tactics and a false pace usually lead to a fiasco as opposed to a true race.

"The only thing we have to fear is fear itself."
– Franklin D Roosevelt.

Distance and Going

The two things that distance and going have in common are breeding. With the exception of sprinters the majority of horses step up in distance as they age - horses develop stamina as they mature.

Some horses can tackle a variety of distances but in the main, each animal has an optimum distance - dependent on breeding not training. Few horses will go on any going, just as a horse has an optimum trip, it also has an optimum kind of going. The going is so important that some horses, who need it soft, will not get a chance to run while the ground is good to firm. Extremes of weather mean that some horses can virtually miss a complete season because of unsuitable ground.

A quick glance at your Profile (racehorses and sires) will enlighten you to a horses potential ability to tackle going and distance and equally important, if the going or distance haven't been tackled before, it will give you a valuable insight of what the horse might achieve on breeding. There is no excuse for not looking at every angle, before placing a bet. A local punter – famous for post-mortems on races that he shouldn't have been involved in, would always blame the going when his horse lost. Never find yourself in that position - if you have to guess about the going then it is definitely a **No Bet** situation. The same applies to distance.

"We have forty million reasons for failure
but not a single excuse." – *Rudyard Kipling.*

Is Speed of the Essence? – Mainly in the U.S.A

Speed is an important factor in racing. Occasionally you'll see a race run so quickly, it will make you gasp. Occasionally you'll see a track's speed record broken - but the operative word is Occasionally.

My thoughts on speed could not be summed up more succinctly than in the following quote from *Ecclesiastes:*

> "And I looked, and I saw under the sun that <u>the race is not to the swift,</u> nor the battle to the strong, nor yet counsel to the wise, nor yet riches to men of skill, nor yet favour to men of understanding,
>
> but <u>time and chance happeneth to them all."</u>

A good speed figure will help on some tracks, and I've outlined these further on in this book. But in many cases, because of the way a race unfolds and pace is dictated - a horse that ostensibly has an inferior speed figure wins the race, often because speedier horses have burnt themselves out against each other, ahead of the eventual victor who comes off the pace.

This doesn't mean that I'm advocating the following of one paced, no hope horses. But I do advocate that, unless the track demands it, speed figures should not be a governing factor in your selection. In contrast, on the dirt tracks in the U.S.A. Speed figures are paramount.

(Also see standard times under the heading of **Irrefutable Form.)**

Inspiration

Having congratulated a jockey on the ride he'd given a horse at Chester, he gave me a wry smile, but was too modest to go into any detail of the manoeuvre he'd undertaken to win the race. Drawn from, impossible, stall sixteen in a sprint, he pegged his horse back, crossed behind the complete field and proceeded to weave his way through alongside the rails, winning the race by a length. No student of form would have backed the horse with this impossible draw at Chester; the horse won at long odds. The jockey in question was one of the very best in the country.

The top few jockeys are capable of magic. Inspired rides like the one mentioned, make it imperative that you stay with top jockeys, they consistently win and so will you. It takes a combination of genius and hard work for a jockey to get to the top. Once you begin to understand the finer points of race riding and the tenacity needed to stay at the top - you will find it impossible to oppose the best with the mediocre.

"Genius is one per cent inspiration,
ninety nine per cent perspiration." – *Thomas Edison.*

The Draw and Other Things

You will often be tempted to back a horse that has a bad draw. Absolutely everything will be in its favour with the exception of the draw. In your Racing Post Weekender which covers racing for Thursday, Friday and Saturday; you'll find a small statistical box for each meeting entitled: Ten-Year Tell-Tale. This breaks down the percentage of winners from high, middle and low draws for each race covering the previous ten years. You will now be able to calculate - if it is worth going against the draw. You might ask what you do about working out the draw on Monday, Tuesday and Wednesday? Hopefully the Racing Post will make this feature available in its daily paper. This Ten-Year Tell-Tale also gives information on profit and loss of first and second favourites, average winning odds, percentage of winners placed in their last three runs, ages of winners in the last ten years, average winning weight and top trainers in each race. As this box only measures 3"x 2" weight for size I would say this is the best information in racing. Returning to the draw, when you get to the tracks section you'll find I've covered the draw. A useful thing to note regarding the draw is this, a horse putting up a good performance, winning or getting placed from a bad draw is at a decided advantage on its next run, if the draw is favourable.

"Flight from temptation is a triumph." – *Spanish Proverb.*

Off the Pace

There's no horse more difficult to quantify than the horse that wins off the pace. Held up behind - the horse is produced to win on the line. These coups can only be trusted to accomplished jockeys, masters of pace and momentum. There's no finer betting medium than a horse of this kind. The horse could well be an improving three-year old, 14lb+ ahead of the handicapper, and - with the right conditions - be ready to win again at will. The *shrewd trainer* has every option with such a horse that can go on to win a sequence of races or be saved for one big coup in the future. When a trainer finds he has a horse of this calibre, he'll take the greatest care in executing his plan.

Dark horses of this kind are few, but it's not difficult to spot a horse winning off the pace and once you do, you have to follow it closely and try to assess which route the trainer will decide to take. In the track's section of this book - tracks that suit hold-up horses are delineated. An off the pace (hold-up) horse that's been running on tracks that suit front runners, and is then returned to a track that suits coming late, can be taken as a significant clue that the horse is ready to win. Of course, this is also true of the front runner, deliberately run on tracks that negate its inherent advantage.

"Coming events cast their shadows before."
– *Campbell.*

Won the Race Last Year

It's always interesting when a horse revisits a track on the anniversary of a win. Some punters will follow such an occurrence blindly and back the horse. Sometimes they repeat their win; more often they don't. The way to look into the horse in question is to look at the runs it had leading up to its win the previous year. If the pattern is much the same and the horse is apparently well-in, you will be able to think seriously about backing the horse. Remembering that it would have already satisfied the **Essential Criteria**. It's also interesting to look into a trainer running a different horse in the race he won last year, to see if this years horse is following the same pattern as last year's winner, and if it is the same age and approximate weight - is last years jockey on board?

While in this area of retrospection; I always look into the form book relating to the equivalent 14 day period last year. It's simple to do, and alerts you to horses and trainers who come into form at this particular time of the year.

"You can only find truth with logic if you have already found truth without it." – *G. K. Chesterton.*

Trainers, Creatures of Habit

It's Important to study trainers, their methods and tendencies. The best way to do this is to focus on one specific trainer, you will soon find that, once you divine the trends of one trainer, you will quickly add further trainers to your repertoire. Some trainers are brilliant with older horses - some excel with horses on their first run - some can produce a horse, race fit after a long lay off. There's no substitute for this knowledge. Don't be daunted by the amount of information you accumulate, as when you're studying a race, you'll have discounted most of the field, before you need to look deeply at a few individual trainers. Invariably, when you come to selecting a horse, information about the type of race a trainer specialises in, will prove crucial.

You need to monitor successful gambling stables - there are certain stables where the value exists in - not getting what appeared to be the value. Early morning gambles that continue on the track can sometimes be worth following. Whereas, following early morning gambles blindly, is the road to Carey Street. You'll soon realise that there are some stables that when the money is **truly** down, it's rarely left behind.

"Most idiosyncrasies, repeated three times, become habitual."

– Maurice Capitanchik.

Follow that Claimer

Virtually every year, a brilliant young jockey appears. You might not be the first to notice him but after a couple of good performances there will be a piece about him in the racing press. This article written in praise of a *rising star* is very important. Firstly to the claimer himself for, if he had a shred of self-doubt, this boost will convince him that, one day he will be *Champion Jockey*. It will also alert trainers with live horses that there's a winning length to be found here, and the claimer will be given every chance to prove his worth. The newspaper article becomes self-fulfiling prophecy.

This is a jockey to follow, without waiting for much further proof, as the party will be over quickly enough, and his value will be reflected in the reduced odds of anything he rides. Regardless that he's a claimer; when riding against his contemporaries in claiming races his mount will be priced as if the outcome of the race is a foregone conclusion. Each ride this claimer is given merits extra scrutiny. He's going to be riding winners and you must give yourself every chance to be on them.

"For we, which now behold these present days,
Have eyes to wonder, but lack tongues to praise."
– William Shakespeare.

Blinkers and Visors etc

The usual reason for applying blinkers or a visor to a horse is to concentrate its mind on running a race. Some front runners fall back through the field the moment they are headed, and blinkers are a definite aid in this instance. Blinkers also come in very handy as an excuse to the stewards when a horse improves beyond recognition, the trainer can insist that the blinkers have worked the oracle. If a horse has been off the track for quite a while and is making a re-appearance in blinkers for the first time don't be shocked to see it win at decent odds, especially if it's the charge of a *tricky trainer*. Blinkers are also very often an attempt to liven up a horse who has lost enthusiasm for the game. As an aid to finding winners, blinkers are not the most consistent guide.

You will see a greater percentage of visors on the All Weather tracks as many of the visors are fitted with Perspex cups which shield the horses eyes from the (sand) kickback.

Tongue-straps are used to help a horse with breathing difficulties. They make a great difference. Once a tongue-strap is applied, problem horses often show dramatic improvement.

"He who knows the road can go at a trot."
– *Italian Proverb.*

Paddock Watching

Many allude to being good paddock judges, few actually are. It's usually a matter of pride, nobody is keen to admit, although they are supposed experts at the game, they don't have a clue when it comes to looking at, or appraising, a horse.

Subsequently, the Kings New Coat syndrome surfaces and many who would be wiser, keeping their counsel, venture some odd opinions. One of the best jockeys in the business once told me that, a horse is much like a sofa, you don't really know much until you sit on it. I'll be the first to admit that my knowledge in the paddock is limited, regardless of intense tuition, by some really good paddock judges, having done little for me. But where I seem to score is when the horses leave the paddock and are going down. If a horse is pulling hard, it will probably have thrown away the race on the way down. A horse struggling to post is a bad portent.

The thing that really gives me a clue of both horse and jockey, on the way down, is the jockey's demeanour. A glance at the jockey's face will usually tell if this is - just another day at the office or more serious business is in prospect. The human face is far easier to read, than the countenance of a horse. The only drawback in watching horses going down is, you can't be in the ring to take an early price.

One horse to another -

"Was that the trainer?" "I don't know, all humans look the same to me!"

Panic + Illusion = Punter Confusion

The casino operators in Las Vegas have a theory that it takes an average of three days for each punter playing the fruit machines to lose $5000. These machines are checked by the Nevada State Commission to ensure that on every $100 of turnover the casinos make *only* a profit of $8. If you consider that U.K bookmakers stand to make more than double this profit, per horse race, the punter might consider losing his money in the more vibrant surroundings of Las Vegas.

For those amongst you who have managed to retain a coin, if you take it out of your pocket and throw it into the air, assuming it doesn't stay up there - and comes back down - there are two chances - heads or tails. This is a true even chance - it's 50% v 50%.

But of course, until it lands, you're in the dark, you just don't know. When a horse in a six-horse race is priced at evens the odds state that the evens horse has a 50% chance of winning the race and the other 5 horses, grouped together, have a 50% chance of winning. Now there's no need for me to tell you that you can toss your coin in the air and while it's still spinning call it wrong quite a few times in succession. In fact - with this true evens shot - runs of six of one and half a dozen of the other are no unusual occurrence.

"A man walks down the street, holds no currency." – *Paul Simon.*

Mathematicians and statisticians thrive on delving into the laws governing probability and they consider tossing a coin a mechanical test. They have also devised mathematical tests showing what kind of losing sequence you might expect with: 2/1, 3/1, 4/1 chances, Ad Infinitum. Their findings reveal that if you are backing a mechanical 4/1 shot, it's statistically proven you will <u>often</u> have runs of over twenty losses going against you. Mechanical chances by their nature cannot be tampered with but who could put their hand on a form book and swear that every horse race is tamper-proof.

The backer of an evens shot has to take the following into account.

(1.) A horse race is far from tamper-proof.

(2.) The evens shot has a built in mark up for the bookmaker.

(3.) In a six-horse race, the bookmaker has five horses running for him.

(4.) In a Hurdle or a Chase the bookmaker has about a 10% advantage of a horse falling, being brought down or pulled up - going against the punter.

In my estimation anyone interested in evens shots should go to the casino and play roulette. It will eminently satisfy the need to lose and because of the speed of the game, notwithstanding that the odds are more in the punter's favour, the painful process is over faster and the punter is then in a position to return to the mundane pleasures of everyday living.

"Money! It tells you if you've done well or badly." – *Donald Trump.*

Fools and Horses

It's important to remember, an evens chance, if all things were equal, which in a horse race they are not, has a 50% chance of winning. Every price on the bookmaker's board represents each horse's chance. I'm not going to bore you with a table of prices and percentages because, at this stage, you only need to know one other percentage; that's the percentage of a 1/2 shot. Looked upon by many punters as an absolute certainty because of its *alluring* short price.

In a horse race, a 1/2 shot would have about a 66% chance of winning. It doesn't need Bill Gates to tell you that, a 1/2 horse has only 16% more chance of winning than an evens horse. In effect you're laying out 100% more to achieve the same result with approx. a 16% better chance of achieving your aim. Theoretically what this tells us is:

Fools, back horses at <u>evens</u> and lunatics, back horses at <u>odds-on</u>.

" If you have the five you don't need the two"
*– This quote is attributed to a U.S sports pundit -
when asked if it was viable to bet on a 2/5 shot.*

"Long ago I came to the conclusion that
all life is 6/5 against." *– Damon Runyon.*

Not So Simple Mathematics

The Bookmaker uses the illusion of fleeting value and barrow boy psychology to entice the punter. The punter has to understand that most of the figures he sees on the bookmaker's board are tantamount to a mirage. Many horses on the board <u>don't</u> get backed - they are notional. What I've illustrated with the evens horse and the 1/2 horse covers the complete spectrum of prices. At the lower end of the pricing scale the bookmaker has it all in his favour. There is a spectrum favouring the punter, these are horses priced between: 5/1 and 9/1. At these prices value can be achieved - value depreciates in both directions as it drops below 5/1 and goes above 9/1.

Personally I rarely have a bet below 3/1 and only in exceptional circumstances would I bet at 11/4. But at the far end of the spectrum I'm looking to find the right horse, because the percentages are relatively in my favour. As we know the difference between a 1/2 horse and an evens horse is approx. 16%. The difference between a 9/1 and a 33/1 is approx. 7% in this area we have to play the bookmaker at his own game. We have to, wherever possible, look for favourites to oppose. By the sheer fact that favourites are the worst value - they create value at the other end of the scale. The shorter the price of the favourite the more value it creates in other horses.

"I don't believe in mathematics." – *Albert Einstein.*

Value depreciates below 3/1 and becomes acute below evens. Interestingly, below 3/1 is the where most bets are struck (pro rata). Therefore, for value we're looking to back bigger priced horses and have to make provision for losing runs - they are part of the game.

Coping with losing runs is easy. You only need to do one thing - stake so well within your means that you feel no emotion at losing. The moment emotion enters the equation you can be assured you are staking too high.

They say that the greatest tip in a tipster's armoury is the ten point maximum. With this bet he can re-coup all of his punters losses in one foul swoop. This bet is usually placed on one of those really short ones that look everything of a winner but happens to have an off day, just when it was expected to produce the goods. My reason for mentioning the ten point maximum or any other kind of maximum - be it five star, gilt edged or blue chip is to tell you to forget them all. If you can't get ahead level staking - you are going nowhere anyway. The effect of stake fluctuation on the punter's psyche is devastating. It's bad enough facing inevitable losing runs without escalating your losses in the hope of getting out of trouble.

> "A man who knows the price of everything
> and the value of nothing." – *Oscar Wilde.*

Each-Way No-Way

It's not easy persuading the punter that each-way backing is far from astute. Looking at the situation from the bookmaker's perspective, will help - in seeing each-way backing for what it is. The bookmaker regards the each-way bet as <u>two bets</u> - a <u>win bet</u> and a <u>place bet.</u> The <u>win bet</u> is simple, you decide a horse can win and you back it to win. Now we come to the schizophrenic element. The punter, in two minds, decides to have a place bet on the horse, contradicting his original win bet.

This is how the place bet contradicts the <u>win bet</u>. In a handicap race with between 12 and 15 runners, horses placed: <u>First</u>, second and third get paid out at a quarter of the odds. On this place bet, if your 16/1 shot comes <u>First</u> you get paid 4/1.Which you'll probably agree is chronic value. If you do agree, we've established that one third of the place bet, actually works against you. Now for horses placed second and third. Can you be assured that it's in the jockey's instructions or intention to ride the horse into a place? Can you be assured that your horse, in attempting to win, puts so much exertion into the race, can then do no better than come fourth or fifth? The punters desired result from this place bet is that the horse comes second or third. In a race of fifteen runners the punter is actually betting that his horse will either be second or third of fifteen. An odd bet indeed!

"Schizophrenia cannot be understood without understanding despair."
– R D Laing.

A Day at the Races

When backing horses you're going to be wrong more times than right. If you're <u>not</u> convinced that your horse is going to win you have every reason <u>not</u> to have a bet.

The each-way bet with 16 runners plus, pays four places; there are many who believe that having an each-way bet in a dead 16 runner race gains them some kind of edge. This can only be another bookmaker's myth. Indeed, if you were to place such a bet at early morning prices, under the assumption that you were in a dead 16 runner race, by the time your race is run, you could well find that at least one horse is withdrawn and your notional, mythical edge has evaporated.

The each-way bet between 8 and 11 runners in a handicap pays only one fifth of the odds a place - which is more chronic value. In my opinion the each-way bet, is the bet that adds insult to injury, and here's the final injustice. You cannot have a place bet with a bookmaker unless you have a win bet as well; in effect you are forced to have a win bet, which needs to lose, in order to be able to even participate in a place bet.

" A child of five would understand this!
go fetch a child of five."
– *Groucho Marx.*

Two Against the Field

We now explore the *taboo* of having two horses running for you in the same race. If you back a 10/1 loser (even staking) you lose one point (all bets worked out tax free) If you back another 10/1 shot in the next race and it wins you've made a profit of 10 points. If you now call it a day, you deduct one point from ten points and you've made a nine-point profit.

For the sake of argument, let's assume that you don't call it a day, after all, *you're holding nine points of profit.* In the next race you back two 10/1 shots having one point on each. Hallelujah! Your horses are clear of the field fighting out a finish. You don't give a damn which one wins (apart from wishing you'd done the forecast) you're ecstatic. You win and collect, eleven points - deduct the two points you staked and you're winning nine points. In effect you've had a 9/2 win, exactly the same as you won, backing two 10/1 shots in the first two races. The main reason that punters don't back two horses in a race is psychological, the thought of one loser in a race is *acceptable* - the thought of two is unthinkable.

> "Many a man is mad in certain instances,
>   and goes through his life without having perceived it."
>   – *Johnson.*

80 over 20 and the Relativity Bank

The punter has to come to terms with losses; as they are a major factor in the equation. Losses cannot be ameliorated by each-way backing or compensated for by elaborate staking plans in an attempt to fine tune the *disasters* of the past with *triumphs* in the future. The sequence of events is <u>random</u> and you have to learn to live with constant uncertainty.

For those who have been backing each-way and staking erratically for years - breaking these expensive habits is difficult. The following is a way of easing out of backing each way: Have an <u>80 over 20.</u> That's an 80% win 20% place bet.

When it comes to staking. Stake **evenly** and work from a 100 point bank. i.e. If your initial bank is £1000 each bet is £10. Simply speaking if your average bet is currently £100. you should be working from a Ten Thousand Pound Bank. This is a <u>Relativity Bank</u> that has a built in Feel Good factor, you're working from well within your comfort zone, runs of losses will not affect your equilibrium, and emotion will not be motivating your next move. If you're tempted to increase your stake to cover past losses, don't contemplate doing this on a horse under 5/1. If you do, you'll be playing *your money* straight into the bookmaker's hands.

"Gambling is the son of avarice and
the father of despair." – *French Proverb*

The Reverse Book

The Reverse Book, can only be performed on course, not in a betting shop. The bookmaker has his overheads - his pitch has a value, so whatever it's worth he's entitled to earn a regular percentage of its value. He has to pay the course for the pleasure of taking your money, and he has all the other attendant expenses of running a business. You in turn have your travelling expenses and you've paid to get onto the course. The bookmaker's expenses are never far from his mind when he decides what prices to offer you.

We're now going to price up a race of 8 runners:

Caveat Emptor Selling Stakes (1.)

"Buyer beware selling stakes."

Horse A:	4/6	=	60%	The percentages quoted here are all
Horse B:	7/2	=	22%	rounded up or down to make them
Horse C:	7/1	=	12%	easy to memorise. At their true
Horse D:	10/1	=	9%	percentage they total 119.3%.
Horse E:	16/1	=	6%	You will find my rounded up
Horse F:	20/1	=	5%	or down figures far easier to
Horse G:	25/1	=	4%	remember, and you won't be
Horse H:	100/1	=	1%	juggling with fractions unnecessarily.
	Total	=	119%	

The Reverse Book entails you making more than one selection in a race. The kind of race you're looking for ideally needs a false favourite. You only have to look at how many odds-on horses get beaten to realise that it's no impossible task to find one.

The favourite in our hypothetical race (1) has been dropped into a selling race - it has one of the best jockeys in the business riding - apart from its last race a month ago, it has impeccable form; and we're always willing to forgive one bad run. The newspapers have made it a 1/2 shot and the bookmakers *seem* to be giving *value* at 4/6.

Every newspaper tipster has tipped the horse apart from one, who always goes against the crowd anyway, but everybody seems to have overlooked two things. The trainer hasn't had a winner for six weeks and he also has a poor record at this track.

You can't really separate horses B,C and D. As far as you're concerned if the favourite doesn't win, either B,C or D will. Meanwhile the punters who fancy the favourite for their lives are thrusting their cash at the bookmakers.

"You know my methods, apply them." – *Sir Arthur Conan Doyle.*

You notice that horse B is 3/1 with one Bookmaker and 4/1 with another. You've made the decision that you're going to back horses B,C and D. And B is the first you're going to tackle.

Your regular bet is £120.

You have £60 to win on horse B. @ 4/1 (£240. to £60)

You have £30 to win on horse C. @ 7/1 (£210. to £30)

You have £30 to win on horse D. @ 10/1 (£300. to £30)

Just at the off you can see that you could have done better as there was some 8/1 available on horse C. but don't worry some of the most astute professionals back this way and they rarely get the best price all round; despite their determination. Had you backed the favourite in this race at the 4/6 offered, you would have stood to win £80. The race begins in earnest and the favourite, a confirmed front runner, does what front runners do. You're having second thoughts. Glancing around, you see that the punters all look very confident and, you can gain no comfort from the poker faces of the bookmakers who have laid the favourite.

"Reason lies between bridle and spur." – *Italian proverb*

Seeing that we can manifest our own outcome to the race, the favourite gets beaten by a short head on the line; in the time honoured tradition of favourites that get beaten. I'll leave you to determine which of the three horses you backed won. You have played partial-bookmaker and given yourself every chance of winning, just as the bookmaker does. Of course you could have juggled your stake about on the three horses you backed, to favour one of the three, and gone for just getting your stake back on the other two. I know of many professionals who make their living by backing around the board in this way, they get value by taking the best prices offered - they make a Reverse Book and, like the bookmaker, are masters of their own destiny. Whereas the punter is more a slave to fashion - a sucker for short priced favourites. Although, many professional punters are successful making a Reverse Book. I have yet to meet a successful each-way backer, or for that matter a Placepot millionaire, but that's another story. By making a Reverse Book you're looking to make a percentage on the race, and in order to make that percentage you must have a fair understanding of what value the odds represent. I continue with another hypothetical race, this one with eleven runners and all of the odds percentages are approx.

"Get on the crupper of a good stout hypothesis,
and you may ride around the world." – *Sterne.*

Audentas Fortuna Juvat Handicap. (2.)

"Fortune favours the brave Handicap"

Horse A:	2/1	=	33%	You add up the percentages
Horse B:	3/1	=	25%	and know, even with the healthy
Horse C:	4/1	=	20%	mark up our Bookmakers enjoy,
Horse D:	11/2	=	15%	141% is steep.
Horse E:	6/1	=	14%	Prices are going to improve
Horse F:	8/1	=	11%	by ten or fifteen per cent,
Horse G:	12/1	=	8%	especially after a few clueless punters,
Horse H:	14/1	=	6%	take some very poor value.
Horse J:	14/1	=	6%	If the favourite and the second
Horse K:	50/1	=	2%	favourite both drift out a point,
Horse L:	100/1	=	1%	the bookmakers will still be
	Total	=	141%	having a party betting to 126%.

The make up of this race doesn't favour the Reverse Book. It's the kind of race where if you strongly fancied a big priced horse it would be a win bet. This over-round book has the first three in the betting totalling nearly 80% - the only thing that might develop here is a gamble on one of the outsiders.

It could well be a horse that you've already ear marked. This is a race for the pragmatic; only those with years of experience should get involved here.

"We are prepared to go to the gates of hell, but no further."
– Pope Pius VII.

Three Weddings and a Funeral

The race you actually came for is the last race of the day - "The Get Out Stakes." You're convinced that the favourite is *no good*, notwithstanding, that he has won his last three races. The horse carries top weight today in a seven runner handicap and the five pound claimer who rode him, in large field handicaps, in his past three wins, has the ride today.

The horse who has risen steadily in the weights, has been raised a further six pounds for his last run, and because the horse is contesting a much lesser grade race than last time, he's shouldering a further eight pound burden in actual weight terms. In effect, the horse is carrying an extra stone in lead - an extra stone in dead weight as opposed to the well balanced weight of a jockey. Add to this the fact that this small but plucky horse, well suited to carrying low weights in big handicaps, will not easily shoulder the extra dead weight. His winning sequence has made him flavour of the month, a short priced favourite in a low grade handicap, and you're sure that this horse can be beaten.

"Measure not by a scale of perfection,
the meagre products of reality." – *Schiller.*

The Aliena Optimum Frui Insania Handicap (3.)

"Best to profit by the madness of others Handicap"

Horse A:	9/4	=	30%
Horse B:	5/2	=	29%
Horse C:	9/2	=	18%
Horse D:	9/1	=	10%
Horse E:	11/1	=	8%
Horse F:	11/1	=	8%
Horse G:	16/1	=	6%
Total		=	109%

The bookmakers are working to 109% on our approx. rating. Something will get backed in. It's an event waiting to happen. The favourite had a good press, with a headline stating that the the four timer is on the cards.

This seven runner 1 mile, handicap looks to the bookmakers as if it's between the first three. You want to back horses B and C and you're hoping that the punters will come for the favourite. If they're fool enough to back in a handicap at 9/4 or less - you've decided to be as astute as the bookmakers. The punters come for the favourite backing it down to 7/4 (= 36% of the book.) With the utmost difficulty you secure 3/1 about B, and 5/1 about C, having £60. on each.

They're off! The favourite gets a good break and tucks itself in behind Horse B. The field strings itself out with horses D to G in alphabetical order followed by horse C, the one that you want to win. At 2 furlongs out - the two in front pull away for a ding dong battle.

"Boot, saddle, to horse and away!" – *Robert Browning.*

One to Oppose Next Time

You notice that the jockey on horse C, your 5/1 shot, hasn't bothered to move a muscle and you wonder if this horse is at the races today. As they hit the furlong marker, the two up front, still neck and neck, run out of steam and come back to the field.

Seeing this, the jockeys on horses D to G start shaking up their mounts, horse C who has never shown any pace in his career appears to be coming to win the race on the bridle but the favourite, as game as the proverbial bagel, makes one last lunge at the line in an attempt to deprive horse C of what appeared to be an effortless win.

The favourite lost (but only just) in actual fact it was the trainer who really lost the race and not the horse. Sentimentality had crept into the equation; the claimer who'd won on the horse three times kept the ride.

Had they substituted the boy for a heavier jockey, the horse would have been carrying more jockey and less lead, and on its performance it would have won. The winner could well be a false favourite for the bookies next time out. It won by default, although it looked as if it was coming there easily and won on the bridle – this was an optical illusion. What actually happened was the rest of the field came back to him.

The opposite of this situation is when a top jockey is riding at his lowest possible weight - always be alert to this positive factor. Jockey's weights appear each day in the Racing Post under seasonal statistics.

"The sentimental by and by will have to give place
to the practical." – *Carlyle.*

As far as we are concerned there are three kinds of races:

A. A race where we fancy a horse strongly enough to back it to win.

B. A race where we want to be with the bookmakers because their book is so biased that the value is in opposing a short priced favourite. You have to be at the track to accomplish the Reverse Book as it is dependant on shopping around for the best price possible.

C. A race where we have no opinion, and avoid as far as betting is concerned, but nevertheless, a race to watch for future reference.

I hope that I have managed to convince you that each-way betting is out of the question. If you've punted for years and are difficult to convince - I will not be surprised, as seasoned punters can be very stubborn regardless of what it costs them. There is of course the more viable alternative of backing a second horse to win. Now we come to multiples, firstly the multiples invented by the bookmakers. Union Jacks, Goliaths etc. and many more waiting to be invented in the future. The bookmakers call these bets "products", and be assured that they wouldn't invent a product unless it was lucrative.

A true professional, there are very few, will go to the track for one horse, win or lose, his mind will be focussed. Anyone having *fun bets* on specialised betting slips concocted by the bookmaker's, that are dependent on sequences of horses winning, will soon forget the true meaning of fun.

"He intended, he said, to devote the rest of his life to learning the remaining twenty-three letters of the alphabet." – *George Orwell.*

Serendipitous

Doubles, Trebles and Accumulators - You can't embark on these bets as a regular feature of your betting. But if I were to tell you to take the serendipity factor out of your life, I'd be selling you short.

I know of a few people, who have had big wins on multiple bets, *"Copped the lot"* as they say in the trade. The time to go in for these multiples is at the big meetings when value is going to exist in most races. Treat multiples as a very separate entity to your regular betting, and keep your stakes to the absolute minimum, also insure you have <u>win</u> multiples. All the talk of each-way doubles being thieving bets etc. is just talk.

Once upon a time, as all good fairy tales begin, the bookmaker's were giving better value on each-way betting. At this time some *shrewd* punters known as *each-way thieves*, lined their pockets. But the bookmakers have been getting their own back ever since. The multiple isn't the most rational bet, but should you deny yourself a chance to dream and not give an Angel a chance to sit on your shoulder, your existence would be sadly diminished.

> " You don't want no pie in the sky when you die!
> You want something here, on the ground, while you're around."
>
> – *Muhammed Ali.*

Money to Burn

Everybody is looking for a panacea - the quick method that gives the outcome of a race in minutes. The punter by his very nature, seeks the easy way out. Punters aren't too keen on working nine to five, in the main they are generally allergic to a hard day's graft.

There is no quick fix - every possibility has to be taken into account when working out the possible winner of a horse race. If you think I'm a little harsh on the punter, then I apologise to the five per cent or so that do put in some effort. But I can't find much sympathy for the other ninety five per cent who live their lives writing betting slips that are destined to be crumpled with aplomb within minutes of being written.

If there wasn't a law about defacing currency, I would invite any punter to take a twenty pound note out of his pocket and put a match to it, as opposed to writing out a betting slip on a whim. In effect there is no difference to the outcome of the punter's money - the crumpled betting slip and the burning twenty pound note are one and the same.

"Believe 95% of what you see and 5% of what you hear -
and that's very doubtful, that 5%" – *William Hill.*

"Riches come better after poverty, than poverty after riches"
– *Chinese Proverb.*

RACING SYSTEMS
CHANGE HANDS
AT £10,000
BOOKMAKERS FILE FOR BANKRUPTCY

If a system worked you would have seen the above headline in the newspapers. There's no doubt that some systems work, some of the time, but no system works all of the time. This of course has little effect on the purveyors of systems - who are always insistent that their system - which only needs your daily newspaper and five minutes of your time - will earn you far more than you're getting working for a living. If there was anything in this; the gross national product would have plummeted to zilch, and we'd be an island of beachcombers - which wouldn't suit any of us who have visited Yarmouth on a rainy day.

Following a method consistently - constitutes a system. Providing you follow it - one element can constitute a system. You could back top weights in handicaps - that's a system. If you wanted a more intricate system, you could back top weights in handicaps, but only on Wednesdays. System followers would be fascinated by the results.

A System for Beating the System

<u>Awareness</u> is the key to finding winners in horse races. Every decent priced winner you will ever find starts with one clue from a repertory of hundreds of possible clues. Once this clue is found your well on your way. Finding the answers to a horse race needs application. Simplified systems which rely on awarding so many points for each positive factor in a horse's past, usually lead to the favourite which you could have found by locating the first horse in the betting. In time, the list of possible clues that you can add to your repertory will increase. As you become more adept, you'll add your own ideas to the equation. To beat the game you'll find every race demands a different system. You will need to be as pragmatic, in changing tactics, as a chess master. This game isn't a five furlong sprint it's a four mile chase over difficult obstacles.

I have a friend who can only be described as a walking form book. It's a useful facility to have, especially when you need to think quickly, but most of us have to make do with the way our cortex is wired up. Einstein recommended that it was best not to clutter the brain with data, just file it where you can find it. If you've never kept a diary, now is the time to start - put your observations on paper. You have to keep a record of horses that you believe are about to win and other information that can easily be forgotten when faced with a continuous barrage of facts.

"Reason is a very light rider and easily shook off." – *Swift*.

Lines of Form

The study of form lines is important. To develop a solid line of form you initially need the structure of a truly run race. Horses that get placed in such a race have to be followed when returning, race fit, to the track. There's only one proviso here. Check that the horse's form doesn't preclude it running within a short period after a race. Some horses only go well fresh and may not show their best form unless they have had quite a lay off. Others can run within a day or so and take advantage of being race fit. A horse that has the ability to run well frequently should be followed, especially when it has been placed second or third in a hot contest, (sprints excepted) as you may have found a *winner without a penalty.*

The trainer's, *modus operandi,* vary as much as their horses. Some will get their horses race fit on the track, others will have tuned them up at home. There are some trainers you would never follow on a horse's first outing of the season and there are others who could have a horse fit to win after a year's lay off. These trainer's traits have to be studied - the amount of early season, false favourites, said to have been, in need of the run, after a race, keep bookmakers in their mansions and limousines.

"Every moment as it passes, is of infinite value,
for it is a representative of a whole eternity." – *Goethe.*

The short cut to finding lines of form is to check on any winning horse that was third or fourth last time out. This will of course throw up a second and a third to that previous race - all you need to do is check if the second or third has been out and won since or - is their win *imminent*? Invest in a packet of coloured high lighters and bring some colour to your form book. This may seem simplistic but you'll be amazed at how much easier lines of form can be followed by colour. Once you've created your own colour code you'll find it difficult working without it. Using your colour coded form book - you will always have a plentiful supply of possible horses whose form has been franked.

Obvious lines of form don't quite apply to sprinters. In any given season on the flat, there are invariably one or sometimes two stables that hold the aces. They have an endless stream of 5f and 6f (2 y.o's) winning. These stables of course have better lines of form to follow than the punter. They know just how well their horses are running at home, and because of the consistency of sprinters they can judge horses against each other off the track. This means that when a horse from one stable beats a horse from a second stable, in a truly run race, the stable that was beaten may not be showing its nap hand. In effect the stables put out horses in these events with more than just the intention of winning a race, often the beaten horse will be a yardstick for the future.

The key to following these hidden lines of form is to specialise in the top stables that are scoring with 2y.o sprinters. You will very quickly gain an insight as to how they sequence their best horses as the season progresses. It's not difficult to keep a list of 5f and 6f horses of the stables of the moment. You will quickly determine the pattern that stables follow in bringing an unexposed horse out to beat an exposed one, due to them having its measure in a horse back at the yard. Even though there might not be a lot of public form for the horse that is up to win, you will be able to determine by breeding and the trainers past record at the track if you're onto a dark horse.

(The above applies to juveniles, 2 year olds, in non handicaps.)

A word of warning about sprint handicappers - it's no secret that these horses appear to take it in turns to win; be assured this is far from premeditated. Sprint handicaps 3 y.o's + end up in more photo finishes than any other races. If you enjoy sweating on a photo, don't let me stop you having a punt. Once or twice in a season a sprinter improves faster than the handicapper can heap on the weight. Hopefully these will be the rare occasions that you back a horse in a handicap sprint. (In Nurserys, handicaps for 2 y.o's, the handicapper is at his best, subsequently, top weights and second top weights in Nurserys have to be scrutinised.)

> "It is a great step in finesse to make people
> underestimate your acuteness." – *La Bruyere.*

Irrefutable Form

Form is about ands, ifs, buts and hidden agendas. It's difficult to concentrate when studying form, when we are constantly questioning and attempting to second-guess the form book. The race reader, limited by the laws of libel, can only say so much. You're not going to read: "It wasn't off an inch!" Explaining why a horse was beaten.

The form book is our map. Adrift at sea, any map may seem preferable to no map! But what use is a map of London's Underground when you're abandoned in the Atlantic?

We have to learn to navigate by the stars and consider only form we believe to be irrefutable. We are looking for truly run races, these are our lode stone. And within these races we are only interested in the horses that contributed a sustained effort.

Although we cannot legislate for what might happen in the future, we must be able to discern what <u>actually</u> happened in the past. In effect we configure an Irrefutable Form book, which concentrates on horses, only when they showed of their best. If only three horses in an eight-runner race - made a race of it - we ignore the other five. There's no point in trying to discern if a horse lost through human decision or equine disposition.

"Our doubts are traitors, And make us lose the good we oft might win, By fearing to attempt." – *William Shakespeare.*

The Irrefutable Form book relates only to horses that were clearly trying. We now have our North Star. We don't have to meander through the land of double think. Ands, ifs, buts and covert schemes are relegated to another category; there's little point in perusing a form book that is a compilation of question marks.

Our irrefutable form book is easy to devise. Using those high lighters again, we go through the form book and take only races run at, or above, the standard time for the track (taking the going into account) and noting which horses truly became involved in the race. You might find in a twelve-runner race that only four horses qualify. In a twenty-runner handicap, only about third of the field may qualify, this is par for the course. (Standard times are listed in the form book.)

Once the form book is marked in this way, you can use the horses (you are convinced tried) as collateral form. (This is the measurement of two horses that have never met in a race, using a third horse that they have both run against as a yardstick)

Your form book now takes on a different aspect, you might have fewer races to draw your information from, and only a few horses in those races that deserve any kind of rating, but you do have an accurate measure. In effect we are using a logical framework for deduction based on observation and data, a tried and tested method.
Aristotle tackled problems this way 400 years BC.

Collateral Form Once-Removed

Collateral form once-removed, is as easy as **A.B.C.D.**

Horse A has run against C

Horse B has run against D

Horse C has run against A & D

Horse D has run against B & C

Horse A & B race against each other for the first time today. Collateral form measures: two horses that have never raced against each other, against a third horse that has met them both. Often, this instance doesn't exist - that's when we use, collateral form once-removed. As the simplistic equation above shows we can gain an insight into the performance of A against B, by how C shaped against D.

As your Irrefutable Form Book develops, you will gain confidence in the use of, collateral form once-removed. You will find it works particularly well in handicaps. It might seem that a simple numerical rating for each horse would make for easier study of the subject, and this is undoubtedly so as it does make things simpler, but it doesn't provide an insight about the dynamic of horse against horse.

> "I've danced with a man who danced with a girl,
> who's danced with the Prince of Wales." – *Farjeon.*

Most winners come from the first four horses in the betting. Once you've located an outsider that you think has the potential to win a race you might find that it has collateral form or collateral form once-removed with one of these four horses. It's not an unusual event in such a race to be looking at a 33/1 shot whose form holds parity with a 7/1 shot. The percentage difference on the odds of these two horses winning is 9%. 33/1 shots win races, especially big handicaps. If you don't back a 33/1 horse, you will never know what it's like to have a 33/1 winner.

This may seem like an overstatement of the obvious, but there are thousands of punters who cannot understand why they have never collected on a big priced winner, and it somehow never dawns on them that they have never actually backed one.

The majority of horses on the flat, improve between the ages of three and five, albeit in fits and starts. The $64,000 question is - how much will they improve and when will the trainer make that improvement public? With horses improvement is very much a family thing, each horse has a built in blueprint of potential improvement. There are exceptions, but they are few. If the sire was a late developer, the odds are well in favour of its progeny developing late too. The trainer of a horse is going to know this and the whole ethos of buying thoroughbreds is to know what you are getting. In effect the trainer usually has a pre-conceived notion about a horse long before it ever reaches a racetrack.

Panamanian Flags

There's nothing like a change of scenery to perk you up! I'm sure you would have heard this adage more times than a jockey has had to miss his lunch to make the weight. It's true of horses too. A move from one stable to another can create some amazing results. A jaded horse, tired of his surroundings and routine, can be rejuvenated under the attention of a new trainer. This is no secret, and following horses that have moved to a new trainer can prove lucrative.

Most trainers covet horses that they think they can improve; its only natural in a competitive business. A horse moving to, what you judge to be, a better trainer, will show improvement regardless of being perked up by new surroundings. Many horses are claimed in claiming races and bought in selling races - there are of course horses that are moved by their owners for one reason or another. If you've been following a horse that you think has had a few easy runs and is due to pick up a race, should that horse - suddenly change trainers - think seriously about backing it. This is an old ploy - but they are the best, a trainer sells a horse privately to another trainer, which is ready to win. Both trainers are in a position to have a touch and the stewards are in no position to ask about the extraordinary improvement, as they would only get the old story about a change in scenery having worked wonders. This practice, of using a flag of convenience, is rare but worth looking out for.

"There's more to Panama than hats." – *Sergei Kuznetzov.*

The Naps Table

This is rich with information. Most newspaper tipsters will tell you that having to put up a winning bet each day is a difficult task bordering on impossible, but the award of "Best Tipster of the Year" is prestigious and can lead to a big increase in salary and offers from other newspapers.

So it's always important to keep an eye on, in-form tipsters at the top of the table as, when on a roll, their confidence increases and the lines of form they are studying usually lead them to further success. The interesting thing about those who reach the top in any given year is, without one or two big priced winners they wouldn't be there. In fact, one year, a specific tipster went from virtually the bottom to the top with a 66/1 shot. Few, if any, Napsters show a profit after tax, as the nap's table is calculated without tax. The truly rich information is at the bottom end of the Naps Table! A bookmaker I know makes a living by doing his best to lay anything that's tipped by the bottom six tipsters in the table, Of course, this emphasises that the bookie is more capable of lateral thinking than the punter.

The selections that the tipsters at the bottom of the table put up are usually littered with false favourites, and it's not a bad place to start looking for a favourite to oppose, when you intend to make a Reverse Book.

"Everything has its beauty, but not everyone sees it."

– Confucious.

Getting on Velvet

Unlike the punter who's invariably out to make a killing, the bookmaker is out to make a percentage. Bookmaking is a fairly incestuous game. Don't think for one moment that the bookmaker, who's paying you out on a 4/1 shot, has lost on the race. He probably had a healthy book earning him in excess of 20%, and he might have also *got on velvet*, in effect backed the horse at 5/1 with one of his compatriots and cheered your horse on, knowing he was on an evens shot to nothing. The dynamic of the betting ring is intriguing and the old hands have seen every machination you could possibly think of. Their stoic indifference is rarely shattered and they feel comfortable with each unfolding catastrophe that befalls the punter.

An acquaintance of mine, an ageing bookmaker, made quite a fortune laying favourites at specific tracks, as opposed to working on the percentage of making a book. Before going to the track, he would take out an insurance policy. He would choose the four races he was going to play in and back the unnamed favourites in four trebles and an accumulator. By playing both sides against the middle, every option was open to him.

My only reason for mentioning this cunning fellow is to alert anyone contemplating a Reverse Book of the possibility of an insurance policy of unnamed favourites in multiples. This can place you in a no-lose situation and if you're lucky enough to get as far as your accumulator paying off - you are in a position to lay the last horse in the sequence.

People in Glass Houses

It is the punter's dream to find <u>The Man</u>, the fellow they telephone everyday, who gives them a certainty to back - which makes them a fortune. They want <u>The Man</u> to convince them that - this is a hell of a good thing, catching pigeons at home, a stone better than anyone might imagine, hasn't been off for its last six runs, home and hosed, etc. etc. etc. The truth is, there are two kinds of tipster - those with half a clue and those who haven't a clue at all. Where do these tipsters come from? All walks of life ex trainers, ex jockeys, ex executives, In effect virtually anything you can put an ex in front of - myself included.

Tipping, good, bad and indifferent has been going on since racing began. In the 1920's, a tipster called Mark Pizzey based at Ascot was <u>The Man</u>, a massive advertiser, he purportedly paid odds-to £50 for a piece of inside information. Multiply this by the rate of inflation and you will find it hard to believe the wads of white fivers that were changing hands. My first venture into tipping was on an 0891 number.
I advertised in the U.K's Chinese Newspapers - with a Chinese interpreter putting on the message - her nickname was Shanghai Rose - she was very popular!

> "The journey of a thousand miles,
> starts with an argument with the wife."
> – *Chinese Proverb*

In the year of writing this book, I've had all the regular ups and downs of the tipster. I started the year by *being done* in a photo on the All-Weather at 33/1. If you're thinking it should have been an each-way bet, you couldn't have been concentrating while reading this book. Amongst my selections, giving only 2 to 3 bets a week, I gave: the winner to the Grand National - BOBBY JO Won at 22/1 > 10/1, the winner to the Welsh National - Kendal Cavalier Won 20/1 > 14/1. (Each was sole bet of the day.) (All bets proofed to the Racing Press.)

If your wondering what happened to my Scottish National Horse -

<u>It's still running!</u>

The tipping game is a great leveller, and you're only as good as your last bet. I only ever give Win Bets and rarely tip a horse at less than 5/1. You might think that I'm lapsing into an advertisement, but I'm not. I'm just stressing the point that I follow my own advice. There's one thing that cannot happen to me, or the clients that follow my phone line; it's impossible for us to suffer the ignominy of a short priced loser; when I'm done in a photo at 33/1, I feel little remorse. Anyone done in a photo at 7/4, or sees their 7/4 shot tailed off, has to suppress a rage within themselves. As it's not the done thing to show emotion in the betting shop or on the track. This pent-up rage gnaws at the soul, leaving a diminished punter haunted by short priced losers.

"It is a clear gain to sacrifice pleasure
in order to avoid pain." – *Schopenhauer.*

Unacceptable Losses

I believe that deep in the subconscious of every gambler is a zone that has the mathematical capability of keeping a running total of every single loss the said gambler has made. In his conscious life these losses are forgotten, as a constant reminder of these losses would hound him to distraction. It is mooted that the average person only uses 10% of their brain power. If this were true, then the gambler would only be using 2% of his brain power with the other 8% occupied with this area of his subconscious that keeps the running total of these *unacceptable* losses.

At the outset this notion may seem a little frivolous to the hardened gambler, but once they think deeply about this, they find a figure surfacing in their conscious mind. This mysterious figure turns out to be exactly the sum they have lost in their gambling career.

The deep-seated need to recoup lost money is sated by the futile playing of catch up. The gambler playing catch up feels momentarily in control while attempting to redress the balance.

Gamblers playing catch up lose every sense of reality. If you were to attempt to talk with one at this point, you would find that they have virtually lost the power of communication.

"A man who has not passed through the inferno of his passions has never overcome them." – *Carl Gustav Jung.*

Catch Up is an Old Game

In financial circles they say that you can judge the rate of inflation by the price of a hair cut. Well I can remember paying the equivalent of ten-pence for a haircut - I don't know the price of a haircut in 1918 but for the sake of argument we'll assume it was 1p. Divide that 1p into the last price you paid for a haircut and you'll have a fair idea of the inflation rate since 1918.

In 1918 at the end of the First World War, J. O. Armour the Packing Case King lost Twenty Million Dollars on the Stock Market, due to changing trading conditions affecting his business. Unable to accept a loss of Twenty Million Dollars, Armour attempted to shore up his business by buying his own stock. He went on to lose his complete fortune, Three Hundred Million Dollars. Armour died bankrupt because making a loss was unacceptable to him. I will leave you to decide on which figure you have to multiply Three Hundred Million Dollars by to work out its current worth, is it? by 500, by 600, or by 1000. Either way we're talking Billions and that's without interest. Armour played *catch up* and lost!

"If you can actually count your money
you're not really a rich man." – *J. Paul Getty.*

The Main Chance

In the 1950's a Stock Market Operative called Darvos wrote a book entitled: <u>How to Make a Million</u>, unfortunately, I no longer have my copy as someone stole it. I wonder if they prospered by it?

The book was mainly autobiographical, but Darvos really did impart his theory on how to make a million. As with all great theories, it was in the main simple and provided the exponent met with fairly good fortune, the theory worked. There's no secret about the Darvos theory, shrewd operators have used it for years and many have made fortunes. The theory fascinated me; I read it at an impressionable age and it was probably one of the factors in me becoming a Stock Market Operative. Darvos didn't believe in portfolios - he believed that: There's only one share to go with, a fast moving share.

Of course, he had his own method of quickly pin pointing which share was out-performing the market - and he would jump on and ride the tiger.

If the share slowed or dropped back, Darvos wasn't afraid to take a quick loss, in readiness to move his capital into the next good thing.

"October! this is one of the peculiarly dangerous months to speculate in stocks. The others are July, January, September, April, November, May, March, June, December, August and February." – *Mark Twain.*

Darvos believed, as I do, that on the Stock Market - a long-term investment is a short-term investment that went wrong. Darvos was only interested in the main chance.

I was in my twenties and Darvos's book sent my pulse racing with the thought of: fast money, fast women and fast cars. Of course I discovered that he who rides the tiger, *often* comes back on the inside.

I'm definitely no believer in that over used cliché. "Only gamble with money you can afford to lose". The kind of money anyone can afford to lose hasn't been invented. But when you're young, if you lose - you at least have time on your side to recoup your losses.

The Darvos theory can of course be transferred to life in general, dead wood is best cut away. If you're intent on making money, the main chance is the only chance. Racing and the Stock Market have much in common - they attract those hungry for cash; and there have been some amazing stories of those who have dabbled in both.

As 98% of punters are net losers, I will assume that most of the punters reading this book have suffered their fair share of losing. But be assured that your losses, although relatively painful, can only border on the insignificant, compared with those of Terry Ramsden. In a five year period Terry Ramsden lost £100,000,000.

Yes! <u>One Hundred Million Pounds</u>, backing horses that lost.

This is no fanciful exaggeration it's all well documented.

Terry Ramsden was a Stock Market Wunderkind of the late 70's and 80's. One who dealt in the exotic area of Japanese' warrants. Without going into great detail, these derivatives were geared in such a way that profits could be compounded faster than the speed of light. At the peak of his city dealing Ramsden, a young cockney of humble beginnings, owned substantial holdings in the largest companies in Japan. Had it not been for the Stock Market Crash in October of 1987 (Black Thursday) "Little Tel", as he was dubbed by the tabloids, might possibly still be losing tens of millions to the bookmakers - who of course - courted his business; so much so, that they employed settlers specifically to deal with his bets. Ramsden became a slave to the buzz. Once you've dealt at the dizzy heights it's virtually impossible to keep your equilibrium. To exist on a day to day basis, ever-escalating chances have to be taken. Terry Ramsden may well have weathered the Stock Market storm had his hobby been fly fishing as opposed to the horses. But it's not all doom and desperation - some punters go on to better things. Sir James Goldsmith left Eton at sixteen on the strength of winning £8000 on a treble at Lewes Racecourse, using that initial capital he went on to make billions on the Stock Market.

"The revolution eats its own. Capitalism recreates itself."
– Mordecai Richler.

Buy, Sell, Bye! Bye!

The spread bet was propagated in the Stock Market. I'm not going into the intricacies of the spread bet - as although I was something of an expert in Traded Options - I'm no expert in spread betting. But there's one factor you must remember, the actual bet you are having is your <u>total</u> possible loss i.e. if your playing at £50 a point and the maximum possible loss is 40 points. In fact you are placing a £2000 bet. Notwithstanding, that you can ameliorate deteriorating positions (Invariably at crippling odds.) You have to understand that these are two very different bets. Always remember, the same gearing that took Terry Ramsden to the top - brought him to rock bottom on Black Thursday.

Open-ended positions are dangerous. This brings us back to money you can afford to lose. Remember! Whatever you think you can afford to lose today - you will think very differently tomorrow.

" Losses are comparative,
only imagination makes them of the moment" – *Pascal.*

The Tracks

The tracks in the United Kingdom are one of the most consequential factors in horse racing. If your horse can't handle the track, your form study has been a wasted effort, subsequently, to ensure that you do not waste time each track has to fulfil certain criteria:

Is it a track where speed ratings matter?

Is it a track where favourites have some kind of chance?

Is it a track where favourites are more readily opposed?

Is it a track that favours the front runner?

Is it a track that favours an off the pace horse?

Is it a track that favours course and distance winners?

Is it a track where form from another track will hold up?

Is it a track that only a handful of jockeys can properly negotiate?

In effect the list is endless and the only way to be certain <u>each day</u>, is to completely <u>refresh your memory</u> about the track in question. Read my observations on each of the tracks, and remember, this isn't a static game, make sure you add your own observations daily for each track.

At the end of this book you will find Track Tables for both Flat and Jumps, they list U.K. tracks from Ascot to York and from Aintree to Worcester. A glance down the tables will give you an idea if your horse will be facing track-features encountered before.

Before a horse satisfies track criteria it must satisfy Essential Criteria

ASCOT / Flat - Right Hand - Galloping - Uphill Finish

Draw: Low numbers in large fields have the advantage.

This 1m 5f + Triangular track is suited to the front runner.

In sprints, scrutinise course and distance winners.

Following favourites in big handicaps at prices of 9/2 and over is a strategy I would recommend.

Don't rely too much on form figures here and note Northern raiders who have run reasonably at Haydock in the recent past.

In non-handicaps if a horse is being touted as favourite on the strength of a good top speed figure - oppose it with the Reverse Book.

AYR / Flat - Left Hand - Galloping

Draw: In large fields - low numbers advantage when ground is soft.

This Oval 1m 4f course suits an off the pace horse.

Oppose favourites in handicaps here.

In non-handicaps, look for horses with a good top speed figure.

BATH / Flat - Left Hand - Galloping - Long Run In - Uphill Finish

Draw: Slight advantage to low numbers in race up to a mile.

This 1m 4f Oval track favours the course and distance winner.

Jockeys who have a good record here - enhance it. Horses coming from nearby Salisbury handle the track well. You can comfortably oppose horses rated top on form in handicaps as they have an abysmal record.

In non-handicaps, horses top rated on speed - do exceptionally well.

BEVERLEY / Flat - Left Hand - Galloping - Uphill Finish

Draw: High numbers in races up to a mile have an advantage, especially in either extreme of going, but by tacking over to the stand's rail in very soft conditions, they can find better ground.

This 1m 3f Oval course very much favours the course and distance winner, with the exception of sprints. In non-handicaps, horses top rated on form do exceptionally well here. When looking for winners in handicaps, oppose top rated on speed.

BRIGHTON / Flat - Left Hand - Undulating - Sharp

Draw: Low numbers in sprints.

This 1m 3f U shaped course - is only ridden properly by a handful of jockeys. Jockeyship is everything here.

In handicaps, the combination of a decent price, good speed figure and top weight - pinpoint winners.

In non-handicaps - oppose favourites that are top rated on form with the Reverse Book, as form gained elsewhere rarely transfers here - with the exception of Lingfield form.

CARLISLE / Flat - Right Hand - Undulating - Uphill Finish

Draw: High numbers in sprints - soft ground negates the draw.

This 1m 5f Pear shaped course sees a high percentage of gambled on two year olds winning. In handicaps oppose horses top rated on form or speed. This is not a course for a horse to be burdened with weight.

CATTERICK / Flat - Left Hand - Undulating

Draw: In sprints high number on soft - low numbers on good.

At this 1m 3f Oval course, follow trainers and front runners.

In early season handicaps, favourites hold their own.

In non-handicaps follow horses with good speed figures.

Ensure your jockey has a good record here.

CHEPSTOW /Flat -Left Hand -Undulating -Long Run In -Uphill Finish

Draw: High numbers in larger fields.

This 1m 7f Oval course is best described as enigmatic.

In non-handicaps, top rated on form and speed do well.

In handicaps, top rated, on form do abysmally.

CHESTER/ Flat - Left Hand - Sharp

Draw: Low draw is crucial. This advantage becomes slightly negated when the ground is soft and the inner section of track becomes mulched.

This is a 2m Pear shaped course for specialist trainers and front runners.

Don't expect Chester form to transfer elsewhere.

Favourites win handicaps here at decent prices.

DONCASTER / Flat - Left Hand - Galloping - Long Run In

Draw: When large fields split into two, use the day's earlier races as a guide.

This 2m. Pear shaped course favours course and distance winners.

Off the pace handicappers win here, but bookmakers win the day.

EPSOM / Flat - Left Hand - Undulating - Sharp - Long Run In

Draw: 6f + a high draw is an advantage.

This is a 1m 4f U shaped course. A fast break is essential in sprints.

In non-handicap races - follow horses top rated on speed figures.

In handicaps - oppose top rated speed figures, vigorously.

Don't expect Epsom form to transfer well.

FOLKSTONE / Flat - Right Hand - Undulating

Draw: High numbers, round course. Low numbers, straight course.

This, 1m 2f Oval course favours top weights in handicaps.

In handicaps and non-handicaps - oppose favourites that gained their
status by being top rated on form.

GOODWOOD /Flat - Right Hand- Undulating- Sharp - Long Run In

Draw: High numbers on round course - negated in the wet.

Low numbers in sprints.

This course turns back on itself, and favours a jockey who knows his way.

It also favours a course and distance winner with the exception of sprints.

Horses that have been placed at Newmarket go on to win here.

In non-handicaps the tail doesn't wag the dog here and favourites win.

In handicaps - form doesn't transfer to the track.

HAMILTON / Flat-Right Hand- Undulating-Long Run In-Uphill finish

Draw: High in sprints and high over 9f.

This is a straight course with a couple of loops coming off it.

Course and distance winners do well here, but this is not the best track to step a horse up in distance. Forget established form here and look for trainers and jockeys that excel at the track.

HAYDOCK / Flat- Left Hand - Galloping- Long Run In -Uphill Finish

Draw: A high draw is an advantage on soft.

This Oval course tests the stamina of horse and jockey on the uphill finish.

In non-handicaps - top rated on form and speed do well.

In sprints look deeply into course and distance winners.

In handicaps form doesn't transfer well here with the exception of Newcastle handicap form.

KEMPTON / Flat - Right Hand - Sharp

Draw: Only significant in soft - watch early races of the day to determine.

This 1m 6f Triangular track has a straight sprint course running through it.

This is a track for the front runner. In handicaps and non-handicaps, top rated on form and top rated on speed make no impact. This is very much a 'who dares wins' track, where trainers with a good record at the track can produce a horse to win, at a half-decent price, after a preparatory Newmarket run.

LEICESTER / Flat - Right Hand - Galloping - Long Run In

Draw: No Advantage.

This 1m 6f Oval track favours course and distance winners (not in sprints)

Southern trainers often give a horse a preparatory run at Salisbury before bringing them here. In non-handicaps, oppose short priced favourites.

Leicester form transfers well.

LINGFIELD / Flat (Turf) Left Hand - Undulating - Sharp

Draw: A high draw is crucial here.

This 1m 2f track needs a horse to keep up with the pace - a decent break here is essential.

On a good day here - a few favourites win and a few favourites lose, punters and bookmakers break even and everyone goes home happy at not having made a discernible loss.

MUSSELBURGH / Flat - Right Hand - Sharp

Draw: High Numbers over 7f. In sprints: stalls stand side low, stalls far side high.

This 1m 2f Oval course favours horses that can handle a sharp track.

A strict following of form here is definitely not advised.

Look out for local trainers with a Dark Horse.

NEWBURY / Flat - Left Hand - Galloping - Long Run In

Draw: High numbers on the straight course.

This 1m 7f Oval track has its fair share of, off the pace horses winning. Form in handicaps doesn't work out here.

To make any headway in non-handicaps, you'll have to oppose popular choices. There's value in making a Reverse Book here.

Remember! Soon after finding one false favourite, another comes along a couple of races later.

NEWCASTLE /Flat -Left Hand-Galloping-Long Run In-Uphill Finish

Draw: On straight course high numbers best - negated in soft going.

This 1m 6f+ Oval track is ideal for the, 'off-the-pace' handicapper, top rated on form and speed figures. Fairytales can come true for form students here, in handicaps - at decent prices too - especially if they're partial to a course and distance winner.

If the shrewd favourite backer (if there is such a thing) can't make a profit here in non-handicaps, then everything I've ever thought about favourite backers is true. Newcastle form can be trusted elsewhere.

NEWMARKET /Flat - Right Hand - Long Run In - Uphill Finish

Draw: No significant advantage.

Rowley Mile 2m 2f + July Course - only a cartographer could explain. You'll find in non-handicaps, that the shorter the price of a talked up favourite here, the more chance it has of being beaten. Therefore, exponents of the Reverse Book will find plenty of value in the rest of the field. In handicaps, plump for favourites in races of eight runners or less. Also scrutinise course and distance winners in all handicaps.

NOTTINGHAM/Flat - Left Hand - Galloping - Long Run In

Draw: Low numbers, slight advantage, on the straight course.

This 1m 4f Oval track favours well-balanced horses.

In handicaps favourites and second favourites hold sway.

In non-handicaps horse rated top on speed have to be followed.

PONTEFRACT /Flat -Left Hand -Galloping -Undulating -Uphill Finish

Draw: Low numbers, on the straight course.

This 2m 2f Oval track favours course and distance winners in longer races. Although the tracks are at odds, Thirsk form translates well here.

In handicaps, scrutinise course and distance winners in small fields.

In Non Handicap races, form horses and favourites suffer a poor fate, creating an ideal situation for the Reverse Book.

REDCAR /Flat - Left Hand - Galloping - Long Run In

Draw: High numbers on the straight course.

This 1m 7f Oval course has a quirky drainage and a horse can encounter two kinds of going in the same race. This means that Redcar form will not always transfer elsewhere on the premise of going.

In handicaps, let your money be the last thing you part with here.

In non-handicaps look to follow favourites - top rated on speed.

RIPON /Flat -Right Hand- Undulating - Sharp - Long Run In

Draw: No advantage.

This 1m 5f track favours the course and distance winner.

Speed and form figures make little or no impact here.

There's money to be made here, opposing abundant false favourites, with the Reverse Book.

SALISBURY /Flat -Right Hand -Galloping-Long Run In- Uphill Finish

Draw: High numbers up to a mile - (except on soft, low numbers)

This looped track is, favoured by trainers as a signpost to better things.

In non-handicaps top rated horses on form do well.

Handicaps here are strictly for the Clairvoyant.

The bonus here is that Salisbury form does transfer well.

SANDOWN /Flat -Right Hand -Galloping -Long Run In -Uphill Finish

Draw: 5f races high numbers (especially on soft) when stalls are - far side.
Low numbers when stalls are on the stand side.

This 1m 5f Oval course favours horses that have run well at Ascot.

Non Handicaps here become something of a Mexican stand off between
punter and bookmaker - with the same wad of notes moving to and fro.
When it comes to handicaps the voice of the people can be heard
cheering loudly as the jolly, or second in, passes the post. Concentrate
on the first two or three in the betting here, as they win. Course and
distance winners and horses that have been placed here recently, must be
doubly scrutinised. Top weights do well.

THIRSK/ Flat - Left Hand - Sharp - Long Run In

Draw: In 5f and 6f races, a high draw is needed, (especially on soft).

This 1m 2f Oval track favours the handicap course and distance winner.
Osmosis finds winners in handicaps here and they go on to win
elsewhere.

In non-handicaps this track cries out for the Reverse Book, on occasion
the bookmakers here have verged on the generous.

WARWICK Flat- Left Hand - Sharp

Draw: No significant effect.

This Circular 1m 5f+ track was purpose built for the front runner.
Forget horses top rated on form in handicaps here. You'll invariably find
the winner of a handicap coming from the first three in the betting.
In non handicaps, decent, recent form is what's needed and you can
oppose the favourite with the Reverse Book - oppose it with passion if it
has done its winning off the pace.

WINDSOR / Flat - Left Hand - Sharp - Long Run In

Draw: High numbers have the advantage - especially in big fields.

This 1m 4f Figure of Eight course, sees horses that have been placed at
local Newbury improving here. In the longer distance races, look for
course and distance winners.
In handicaps, top rated on form and speed lose; confounding the experts
and infuriating the punter. To find Handicap winners here you have to
look deeply into the possible, as opposed to what appears definite.
The biggest clue is scrutinise the top weight first, as they win here.
In non-handicaps this is very much a track where the break-even boys
put a lot of effort into breaking even.

YARMOUTH/ Flat - Left Hand - Galloping - Long Run In

Draw: High Numbers best on the straight course.

This 1m 4f Oval course, has left many backers in Handicaps, disillusioned, but in Non-Handicaps it's a favourite backers paradise. Traditionally a weak market, well fancied two year olds get backed into favouritism and win.

If you're a backer of short priced favourites (you have my condolences) ensure that your short priced favourite has a good speed figure, as that is what is needed here. Placed horses from Newmarket go on to win here, albeit at abysmal odds.

YORK /Flat - Left Hand - Galloping - Long Run In

Draw: Advantage to low numbers in sprints, especially on soft going.

This U shaped 2m course favours the course and distance winner. Winners here, go on to win elsewhere - as York form is solid.

In handicaps course and distance winners will give you the feeling of deja vu. This is the best place to crack big handicaps. Horses are laid out to win here - delve a little into their form - you'll soon see which horse is about to improve out of all recognition. Horses win handicaps here at big prices, so you'll be rewarded for your endeavours.

In non-handicaps, winners and placed horses from Newmarket go on to win here.

Before a horse satisfies track criteria it must satisfy Essential Criteria

AINTREE - N/H - Left Hand - Galloping - Stiff Fences

Comprises of two courses: The Grand National course 2m 2f is flat with stiff fences and a long run in. The Mildmay course 1m 3f+ is flat with conventional fences.

This is the home of the greatest racing spectacle in the world - The Grand National. The stiff fences are the tallest and most solid in Christendom, although the Czechs might argue with this, as their Grand National the Velka Pardubicka is another awesome spectacle.

Regardless of how stiff the fences are around Aintree, the hurdles are quite commonplace, and many people tend to forget this. Although there aren't that many hurdle races here, form horses with a decent speed figure have to be scrutinised in handicap hurdles, and favourites opposed.

In chases, both handicap and non-handicap: the market gets it reasonably right with not much leeway for profit, as favourites and second favourites make a decent showing. Improving horses, not burdened with too muchweight should be followed at this course.

Follow fresh horses here that haven't run at Cheltenham.

ASCOT - N/H - Right Hand - Galloping - Uphill Finish - Stiff Fences

This 1m 5f+ track is Triangular with a very short run in. Novice hurdlers who have performed well here on the flat are to be noted.

When the ground is soft, this track is a true test of stamina.

In long distance, non handicap chases, think deeply before opposing the favourite as their strike rate is as formidable as their price is poor.

If the favourite is a front runner it will have an added chance of winning.

Look for a good speed figure in handicap chases as the galloping nature of this track invokes truly run races.

In hurdles races and more so in non handicap hurdles, oppose favourites.

If you've got it in mind to make a Reverse Book, here's the place to start as you'll find the strong betting market gives you a crisp edge.

AYR - N/H - Left Hand - Galloping

This track, just under 1m 4f is Oval. There's a short run in here. If your horse isn't in touch coming over the last couple of fences, tear up your ticket.

In non-handicap chases a decent speed figure doesn't go amiss, and at over three miles, favourites consistently come into the reckoning.

In non-handicap hurdles, favourites actually show a profit - but it's tight.

BANGOR N/H - Left Hand -

This is an Oval course of 1m 2f.

This course is flat enough for the Flat Earth Society to hold meetings here.

If you can find a course and distance winner, with a decent speed figure in a handicap chase - you might be on the verge of considering a bet.

CARLISLE - N/H - Right Hand - Undulating - Uphill Finish

This 1m 5f track is Pear shaped.

Stamina and fluent jumping are needed here to take the last three fences on rising ground. If you latch onto a front runner in a handicap chase with a decent speed figure, you will be making a move in the right direction.

CARTMEL - N/H - Left Hand - Undulating

This is a very tight 1m Oval course and, when they brush the cobwebs off it a couple of times a year, it suits the front runner.

Back favourites in chases here, and oppose favourites over hurdles. Don't follow top weights here.

CATTERICK - N/H - Left Hand - Undulating - Sharp

This 1m 3f. Oval, undulating and sharp track favours the small nippy horse,but don't be lulled into thinking a good speed figure means much here - as it doesn't. The best advice I can give you here is - follow trainers with a good record at the track in handicap hurdles and favourites in the longer distance handicap chases.

CHELTENHAM - N/H Left Hand - Undulating - Uphill - Stiff Fences

This is The Jumps course, 1m 4f+ Oval in shape, with a four furlong, uphill finish, reserved for - none but the brave.

In handicap chases you can go for a good speed figure.

Horses are laid out to win here, subsequently their previous form will not be of much use to you. Top weights struggle here as their unexposed counterparts come in for all the glory.

They call this the punter's graveyard, and many a bookmaker has made enough money at the festival to keep them going for a year or two.

The best advice I can give you is, don't follow any horse immediately after it's been to Cheltenham as it takes months to recover from the arduous, four furlong, uphill finish.

CHEPSTOW -N/H -Left Hand -Undulating -Long Run In -Uphill Finish

This is a 1m 7f+ Oval track where front runners hold their own.

When the going gets heavy, weight becomes an impossible burden here.

In handicap chases, the top rated horse on form can be followed.

Speed figures can be ignored in both handicap and non-handicap chases.

In hurdles, the favourites have to be laid and if you can see an opening for the Reverse Book - become a face and make a name for yourself.

DONCASTER - N/H - Left Hand - Galloping

This, 2m flat track is Pear shaped.

The long striding horse with something of a cruising speed is favoured here over these, not that difficult, fences.

A good front runner poaching a lead can hold onto it here.

Don't oppose favourites in non-handicap chases.

Definitely oppose a good speed figure in a handicap chase.

EXETER - N/H - Right Hand - Undulating - Uphill Finish

This, 2m track is triangular.

Course and distance winners go well here.

A horse with a good speed figure in a non-handicap hurdle or a handicap chase, at a decent price, is what's needed here.

FAKENHAM - N/H - Left Hand - Undulating

This small, 1m square track, favours the front runner.

This is an excellent track for opposing favourites, especially, in handicap chases and if the favourite is carrying top weight - oppose it vigourously. This is not a track for a horse to be burdened with weight.

FOLKSTONE - N/H - Right Hand - Undulating

This 1m 2f pear shaped track - needs a horse to be up with the pace as the short run in can easily catch out the horse with distance to make up. In non-handicaps, hurdles and chases, favourite backers hold the sway but get little for their efforts as prices are poor.

FONTWELL - N/H - Left Hand

Two courses (1m circuit) are superimposed on each other here, a Figure of Eight (the chase course runs both left and right handed) is superimposed on the hurdle course which is Oval shaped.

In non-handicap hurdles, look for priced horses with decent speed figures. In handicap chases, back favourites (advisedly).

Front runners persevere here.

HAYDOCK - N/H - Lft. Hand - Galloping - Lng. Run In - Uphill Finish - Stiff Fences

This, 1m 5f course is Oval shaped and probably second only to Aintree for big drop fences, and that would only be a marginal second.

Don't bother with horses that have the odd fall in their history here.

Follow horses, top rated on form in handicap chases.

HEREFORD - N/H - Right Hand - Stiff Fences

This is a 1m 4f Square track, with one awkwardly placed fence approached on the turn. Horses that find it difficult to jump and turn right at the same time, shouldn't come to Hereford.

Follow favourites in handicap chases here.

In handicap chases also scrutinise the top weight - they win here.

HEXHAM - N/H - Left Hand - Undulating - Uphill Finish

This, 1m 4f Oval track, is prone to extremes of going.

Front runners with the stamina to stay on - win races here.

HUNTINGDON - N/H - Right Hand

This, 1m 4f Oval track, is a fast track with easy fences.

There appears to be no decisive trend to profit from here, either as a punter or layer, the margin is tight all the way round.

KELSO - N/H - Left Handed - Sharp - Uphill

This 1m 1f Oval course suits the front runner, until it comes to the last 500 yds. Then it's usually all change up-front.

You need an off the pace horse here.

Form holds up well here in handicap chases and non-handicap hurdles.

Favourites in non-handicap hurdles are better not opposed.

KEMPTON - N/H - Right Hand - Sharp

This 1m 6f Oval course does not favour the front runner, as much as punters seem to think - they are swayed by the fact that front runners do well here on the flat. In non-handicaps, chases and especially hurdles, favourites succeed. Oppose good speed figures in handicap chases and handicap hurdles.

LEICESTER- N/H -Right Hand -Galloping -Long Run In -Uphill Finish

This is a 1m 6f Oval course. The tight bends, I assume, are the reason that you can dispense with speed figures.

Form doesn't count for much either. There is a living to be made here, opposing false favourites with the Reverse Book, in non-handicap chases, non-handicap hurdles and handicap hurdles.

LINGFIELD - N/H - Left Hand - Sharp

Leafy, as it's known in the trade, this is a 1m 2f furlong, front-runner's paradise, with a short run in to ensure victory.

For those who like a short priced favourite, this is the place to come. I've heard of one or two shrewd punters, who managed to break even here.

LUDLOW - N/H - Right Hand

This is a 1m 4f Oval course and the fences come close to being stiff. The long run in usually sees the false favourites in handicap hurdles struggling home while the exponents of the Reverse Book count their money.

MARKET RASEN - N/H - Right Hand - Undulating

This 1m 2f track is Oval shaped.

The chase fences are on the easy side; but here comes the rub; the second from last has no bearing on the rest, and jockeys who lapse into complacency come a cropper at this exceptional obstacle.

Many a good front runner has come over the last without ever knowing about the mayhem taking place behind, at the second from last.

Latch onto a horse with a good speed figure in a handicap hurdle or a non-handicap chase. When it comes to the Reverse Book, oppose false favourites in handicap hurdles as they're not difficult to find.

MUSSELBURGH - N/H - Right Hand - Sharp

This Oval, 1m 3f track favours the front runner.

Horses top rated on form and favourites do well in handicap hurdles - it's a generous betting market and subsequently favourites can be followed.

For the purposes of the Reverse Book, oppose false favourites in non-handicap chases, as they are abundant.

NEWBURY - N/H - Left Hand - Galloping - Long Run In

This 1m 7f Oval track usually sees long time front runners headed on the long run in. A good speed figure pays dividends in non-handicap chases and handicap hurdles.

(form figures hold little sway in handicap hurdles).

Oppose false favourites in handicap chases.

NEWCASTLE - N/H - Left Hnd. - Galloping -Lng Run In -Uphill Finish Stiff Fences

This 1m 6f course is Oval verging on the Triangular.

Newcastle form holds up and can be followed elsewhere.

Good speed figures can be followed here in handicap and non-handicap chases.

Favourites can be followed in handicap hurdles and non-handicap hurdles.

Another anomaly of this game is, the harder a track looks the easier it is.

NEWTON ABBOT - N/H - Left Hand - Sharp

This 1m 2f Oval track might have been constructed for the front runner. The rewards are high for finding a false favourite here as good things go off at very short prices, ensuring value in the rest of the field.

PERTH - N/H - Right Hand

This 1m 2f Oval track, suits the front runner - but beware of any horse that has shown a tendency to hang left as after the first circuit there's an acute right turn.

Handicap chasers and handicap hurdlers with good speed figures win here at decent prices. In these very same handicaps, avoid horses that appear well in on form. You can make a Reverse Book here by opposing favourites in handicap hurdles if they're also top rated on form.

PLUMPTON N/H - Left Hand - Undulating - Uphill Finish

This 1m 2f Oblong track, suits the well balanced, front-runner.

Top rated form horses win handicap hurdles here.

Course and distance winners have to be doubly respected.

Forget the Reverse Book here as margins are tight.

SANDOWN - N/H - Right Hnd - Galloping -Long Run In - Uphill Finish Stiff Fences

This Oval 1m 5f track - finds out front runners and sees them coming back to the field. If, in effect, a front runner succeeds here, its success will be virtually assured elsewhere as Sandown form can be trusted. Horses with good speed figures do well in handicap chases and handicap hurdles. Top rated horses on form, excel in non-handicap chases.

SEDGFIELD - N/H - Left Hand - Undulating

This 1m 2f Oval course (has a 500ft. run in for chases)

Front runners do well here in hurdles as the run in is only 200ft.

The only strategy I would recommend here is: In handicaps, chases and hurdles, if the favourite also happens to be top rated on form - oppose it with the Reverse Book.

SOUTHWELL - N/H - Left Hand

This 1m Triangular course is reasonably featureless.

If anyone has a strategy here, I'd be pleased to hear about it.

STRATFORD - N/H - Left Hand

This 1m 2f Triangular course has a short run in which finds out any jockey who leaves it a little late. Many favourites in handicap hurdles and handicap chases seem to find themselves in this regrettable position. Non-handicap favourites don't fare any better.

Subsequently, this is an ideal place for the Reverse Book.

TAUNTON - N/H - Left Hand

This 1m 2f track is Oblong -

In handicap chases oppose favourites wherever possible;

horses, top rated on form get turned over in these events.

TOWCESTER - N/H - Right Hand - Galloping - Uphill Finish

This 1m 6f track is Square and boasts an uphill finish of nearly a mile.

The three things a horse needs here are - stamina, stamina and stamina.

If your horse hasn't got a stayer in its family tree - forget it.

UTTOXETER - N/H - Left Hand - Galloping

This 1m 3f Oval track is a haven for favourite backers in

handicap chases.

With patience and this one piece of information you are in a position

to profit at this track.

WARWICK - N/H - Left Hand - Sharp

This 1m 5f+ track is Square verging on the Triangular, a horse with a

galloping action will not get the opportunity to get into its stride.

In non-handicap chases and handicap chases, if the favourite is a front

runner, it needs to be respected as they win here.

WETHERBY - N/H - Left Hand - Galloping - Stiff Fences

This 1m 4f track is Oval and reasonably flat.

Jumping is the name of the game here. If a horse has a fall or two in its history - you'll see history repeat itself here.

In handicap chases oppose favourites. If the favourite is top rated on form, speed or both - oppose it vehemently as form and speed doesn't supply the answer in handicap chases.

WINCANTON - N/H - Right Hand

This is a 1m 3f Oval track - There's a 200yrd uphill run-in that makes for some interesting finishes. Following favourites in non-handicap hurdles, is the only advice I can offer (providing you've Eliminated the Negatives).

WOLVERHAMPTON - N/H - Left Hand - Galloping - Stiff Fences

This Pear shaped 1m 4f course suits stayers.

Since jumps racing only resumed here recently, there's not enough statistical evidence to make a case for any strategy.

WORCESTER - N/H - Left Hand - Galloping

This 1m 5f Oval track is as flat as a pancake.

Sometimes this track actually becomes part of the River Severn.

In handicap chases follow horses top rated on form.

In handicap hurdles generally disregard horses top rated on speed.

CLASS.

I have not graded each individual track by class, as the class of each race is what matters and this is easily determined by the grade of the race. (Races are generally rated from A to G) but the determining factor of the intrinsic value of a race is the prize money on offer, and this is simple to determine from race to race.

Before a horse satisfies track criteria it must satisfy Essential Criteria

The All-Weather Tracks

The All-Weather tracks, LINGFIELD, SOUTHWELL AND WOLVERHAMPTON, are synthetic tracks. In effect they are made up of ersatz sand. The draw is important on these tracks, but like the sands of the desert, it's always changing. Unlike the desert, it's not the wind that changes its contours but the tractors that harrow the courses. The same common sense that applies elsewhere works well here and there are a few simple rules to follow. Southwell and Wolverhampton favour horses that like soft going, but never back a horse at any of the All-Weather tracks that hasn't been tried on the surface. Lingfield favours horses that prefer good or good to firm ground. When the rain hits the All-Weather tracks the sand compacts and makes for a firmer not a softer surface. Don't make any judgements early in the season on the All-Weather, until form settles down. At the beginning of the turf season, horses that are race-fit from the All-Weather - have an added advantage on turf. Horses top rated on speed do well in sellers at both Southwell and Wolverhampton. Follow specialist trainers at these tracks. There's a big future in All-Weather racing - don't underestimate it for a moment.

"To see the world in a grain of sand, And a heaven in a wild flower, Hold infinity in the palm of your hand, And eternity in an hour"

– William Blake.

Meanwhile Back at the Track

Once you're at the track I'm going to assume that you have come up with one or at the most, two selections. The professional thing to do now is to get the best price, this will come with experience. Assuming you're having £100 to win on Moonbeam at 5/1, the correct way to place this bet at the track, and to avoid any confusion afterwards is to say: "£500 to One, Moonbeam". The bookie will repeat this and give you a ticket. If your bet is £200 at 5/1 you say: "£1000 to Two, Moonbeam", which the bookie will repeat. If you just miss the price and have to take 9/2, you'll ask for: "£900 to Two, Moonbeam" which the bookie repeats and gives you your ticket. At the outset you're going to feel uneasy placing your bet this way, the reason being, you are saying - <u>One</u>, as opposed to - <u>One Hundred</u> but the bookmaker is well versed in his art and will understand exactly what you want. With the advent of computerised betting on track, your ticket will put you beyond any doubt that you've placed exactly the bet you intended.

"Proper words in proper places,
make the true definition of a style." – *Jonathan Swift.*

The Vernacular

I had the pleasure of knowing Stubby Kaye who played Nicely Nicely, a Damon Runyon character, in the film Guys and Dolls. The part could have easily have been written with Stubby in mind. In real life, his staccato delivery of the vernacular was amazing. Of course Stubby played more than one Damon Runyon part and it is not difficult to understand how Runyon's colourful language seeped into Stubby's persona. Once involved in racing the language of the track will permeate your conversation, much as it has pervaded this book. The following is something I wrote some years ago illustrating the esoteric nature of racing language. (The mystique of the patois.)

"I had three pony doubles and a pony treble, then I had a bottle on the short priced jolly in the next race, and before you know it I'm doing a carpet. Still it's not all that bad, by this time yesterday I was doing a monkey, which made it a long on the week.

The Jolly = The Favourite, Pony = £25., Doing = Losing, Bottle = £200., Carpet = £300., Monkey = £500., A Long = £ 1000.

"These citizens are always willing to bet that what Nicely Nicely dies of will be over feeding and never anything small like pneumonia. For Nicely Nicely is a guy known far and wide as a character who likes to commit eating." – *Damon Runyon.*

If Damon Runyon could have met Shaw's Prof. Henry Higgins, for the purpose of deciphering race track slang from Aqueduct to Ascot it would have made for an interesting exchange. Track talk is a world-wide phenomenon. In Baden Baden a punter who has no known financial support is know as a Luftmensch = someone living on thin air.

At Longchamp a punter of the same ilk is known as a Lempert.

The following is a pastiche of some of the more obscure racing jargon:

"I wouldn't have a score of quids on it. I had it no good last time it ran, it's supposed to be a bit of a dog. I've heard there's good money for the favourite, I'm sure it was got at last time, I seem to remember there was a bit of a dairy about it that day, but a very warm mob are on today who don't often leave it behind. I'm taking an early price, because one or two faces at the track are sure to know about it."

Score of quids = £20. No good = Negative message for horse.

A dog = Difficult horse to handle. Got at = Horse was stopped.

Good money = Money from the right quarter not to be confused with

"Big money" which is a lot of money and of far less consequence.

Dairy = Suspicion. Warm mob = People in the know.

Faces = Recognisable people in the know.

"The golden rule is that there is no golden rule"

– *George Bernard Shaw.*

Talk Money

There's another angle to be exploited at the track and that's the **FRACTIONS**. They work out like this:

at 11/2 ask for a £500 to Ninety.............Or £1000 to One-eighty.

at 6/1 ask for a £500 to Eighty...............Or £1000 to One-sixty.

at 13/2 ask for a £500 to Seventy-five...Or £1000 to One-fifty.

at 7/1 ask for a £500 to Seventy.............Or £1000 to One-forty.

at 8/1 ask for a £500 to Sixty.................Or £1000 to One-twenty.

at 9/1 ask for a £500 to Fifty-five. ....Or £1000 to One-ten.

at 11/1 ask for a £500 to Forty-five.......Or £1000 to Ninety.

at 12/1 ask for a £500 to Forty..............Or £1000 to Eighty.

at 14/1 ask for a £500 to Thirty-five. ....Or £1000 to Seventy.

at 16/1 ask for a £500 to Thirty. ....Or £1000 to Sixty.

In most of these instances, when you win you're about £40 better off per £1000 worth of winnings. Don't feel demeaned about requesting this edge. Bookmaker's trade between themselves in this way, as they invariably don't *pay on* (pay up front) with each other and only have to settle any winnings. Which of course is much easier when it's in round figures of £500, £1000, £1500 etc. Not that the bookmaker's approval is needed - but he'll be less inclined to think you a mug punter if you have the savoire-faire to <u>talk money.</u>

...About Sidney Harris,

Sidney Harris became interested in horse racing in his
mid-forties. Prior to becoming a full time professional gambler,
Sidney was involved in the Stock Market - trading in options.
Although Sidney's biggest gamble netted over £300,000.
The Stock Market gamble that proved his acumen was on
19/10/87. Black Monday - The Stock Market Crash,
when so called "Financial Advisers" sat frozen at their
VDU screens losing fortunes. Sidney had a bet at mid-day,
certain that the market would continue to free-fall and that
the general panic would continue:

Sidney bought 20 Nov. puts for . . . .£27,500.

Selling them 24 hours later for . . . .£90,000.

Since retiring from the Stock Market, Sidney has devoted his
time to Racing - developing the best contacts in the business.

> " It doesn't matter where you get on the train
> as long as you stay on the train." – *Henry Ford.*